TOM OTTER AI
SLAYING OF MARY KIRKHAM

A 1904 photograph showing the Fossdyke at Saxilby. The swing-bridge across the canal is an early Victorian replacement for the drawbridge that was in use when the events of November 1805 took place. The Sun Inn (then the Sun Hotel), is to the left of the bridge with a carriage stood outside.

Looking along the Fossdyke at Saxilby it is easy to imagine the terrible events that took place nearly 100 years before this photograph was taken. The crowds gathering to see the arrival of the body of Mary Kirkham, and later, the people coming together to see the body of the executed Thomas being taken to the gibbet.

TOM OTTER
AND THE
SLAYING OF MARY KIRKHAM

IAN MORGAN

ASHRIDGE PRESS

Published by:
Ashridge Press/Country Books
Courtyard Cottage, Little Longstone, Bakewell, Derbyshire DE45 1NN
Tel/Fax: 01629 640670
e-mail: dickrichardson@country-books.co.uk

ISBN 978 1 901214 38 3

ACKNOWLEDGEMENTS

Without doubt, the byword for anyone writing a book is co-operation and assistance and there is no doubt that I am indebted to many people for their assistance in the production of this book. Particular thanks must go to Clive Holliday, John Taylor and John Wilson for their valued assistance. I must also thank the staff of Lincoln Castle for their help, and my especial thanks go to the Nottinghamshire Archives for allowing me to reproduce copies of entries taken from within the Tresswell parish register and to the Lincolnshire Archives who have also given permission for the reproduction of entries taken from the parish registers of South Hykeham and Saxilby.

Printed and bound in England by Digital Book Print Ltd.

DEDICATION

To my wife Angela, Clive Holliday and John Taylor
for their unwavering support

The Otter Family Tree

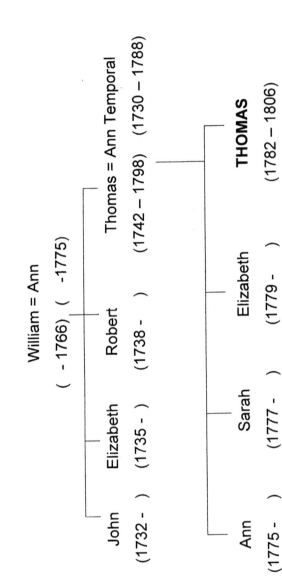

William = Ann
(-1766) (-1775)

John (1732 -)
Elizabeth (1735 -)
Robert (1738 -)
Thomas = Ann Temporal
(1742 – 1798) (1730 – 1788)

Ann (1775 -)
Sarah (1777 -)
Elizabeth (1779 -)
THOMAS (1782 – 1806)

INTRODUCTION

The nineteenth century legend of Tom Otter and his brutal slaying of Mary Kirkham on their wedding day has gone down in history as one the most senseless and violent acts to have taken place against a defenceless woman. The very mention of his name in some quarters brings a shudder to those close by and even the passing of time has failed to heal the wounds that some feel towards him and his wicked act. Throughout his time in the public eye there has been confusion as to his true name. Should he be called Thomas Temple, Temporal, Temporel or Temporall, or is his true name really Thomas Otter? Indeed all through his liaison with Mary Kirkham he took one of the former names and it was not until after his death that it became clear his real name was Thomas Otter. The different spellings of Temporal and the use of Temple arise from his inability to read and write and it was up to the keepers of the various records to decide on how to spell the name that he gave them. But why not use his real name of Otter? That will become clear as the

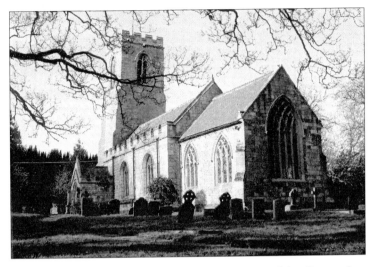

Treswell Church where Thomas Otter (senior) married Ann Temporal, and all their children, including young Thomas, were baptised.

The gravestone of Ann and Thomas Otter in Treswell churchyard.

8

The headstone of William Temporal in Treswell churchyard.

Side by side at Treswell are the graves of William Temporal and those of Ann (nee Temporal) and Thomas Otter.

story unfolds, and as we look into his twisted mind the reasoning behind his cruel acts may become a little clearer. Because Thomas Otter used so many names in the last part of his life I have decided to refer to him simply as Thomas.

To understand the events leading up to the death of Mary Kirkham we must travel back in time to before Thomas was even born. His father, also called Thomas Otter, was born in 1742 and lived as a farmer in Treswell near Retford in Nottinghamshire, coming from quite a large extended family that lived in the locality. Although the family seemed to have been well-established within the community, records seem to show that they only came to the area about a generation earlier. It was not until he was in his thirty-third year that he met and became involved with his future wife, Ann Temporal. Also from a farming family, Ann was older than Thomas by twelve years, and came from a family that had lived locally for many generations, with no less than three of her relatives having been Clerks to the Parish, each member succeeding to the position when their predecessor passed away. Whether Ann was flattered that a younger man was chasing after her or it was a case of an older woman leading a younger man astray no-one will ever know. The facts are that on July 30th 1775 Thomas Otter senior and Ann Temporal married, he at the age of thirty-three she at the age of forty-five, neither of them having been married before. The reason for the marriage was most probably not love, at least not at the outset, for within weeks Ann had given birth to their first child who they also called Ann. Whatever the reasoning for their marriage, love must have blossomed within the relationship, for soon more children

Two views of Treswell village, near Retford, as it is today.

came along. Next to arrive was Sarah followed by Elizabeth and lastly came Thomas, born in the winter of 1782 when his mother was fifty-one years old. A ripe old age to give birth even by modern standards. At his christening how could the Parish rector, who had the magnificent name of Seth Ellis Stevenson, know that the innocent baby he held in his arms would one day grow up to be such a murderous, vile human being whose name would live for evermore in infamy. When he was just six years-old his mother died and Thomas and his sisters were left to be brought up by their father. Perhaps this is why he grew up unable to read or write, for although his mother was illiterate, his father was well able to study and understand books.

Given the constraints of a single parent and having to tend a farm to keep his family, time must have been very limited for Thomas senior. No doubt young Thomas and his sisters had to help on and around the farm from an early age

and academic skills would be low on the scale of priorities.

Ten years later in 1798 Thomas senior died leaving young Thomas to be brought up by one of his uncles. The formative younger years of childhood can forge the character of an adult and perhaps the harsh and difficult early years of the young Thomas helped to lead him down the path of self-destruction. Whatever the reason, there can be no excuse as to the butchery that he was to mete out to the unfortunate Mary Kirkham. So read on and discover the legend of Tom Otter,

Map of the Saxilby area showing the principal sites

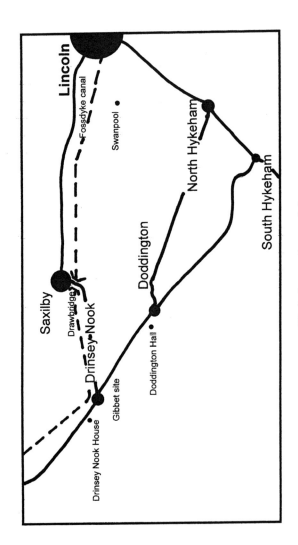

(Not drawn to scale)

TOM OTTER

AND THE SLAYING OF MARY KIRKHAM

The inside of the church at South Hykeham seemed very cold and sombre on this third day of November 1805. Soon the events of this day would chill the blood of local God-fearing people as much as the cruel cold winter to come. Only a few short days earlier Nelson had won his famous victory off Cape Trafalgar. Now the locals would soon have another topic of conversation.

Thomas Brown, the curate of the church at South Hykeham looked at the four lined up in front of him. The two men at the sides he knew, they were the Shuttleworth brothers, John and William, both local constables. The man and woman between them were new to him but he knew full well why they were there. He knew the law as well as any man, the woman was pregnant with the man's child and he had to marry her or go to gaol until he came to his senses and made an honest woman of her. So why put off the event? Marry her now and get it over and done with. The curate eyed the man, he was about five-foot-nine tall, of a stout build and obviously a man of strength. Indeed he was, un-beknown to Brown, the man was a navvie working in Lincoln at the enclosure of the old Swanpool and years of hard work had built up his natural strength. Solemn and uncaring, he had been in custody for the last two days after the Magistrates had found him guilty of the charge of Bastardy, and to make sure he kept his unwelcome appointment, the constables had brought him to the church

South Hykeham church. The scene of the enforced marriage between Mary and Thomas that was to have such tragic conaequences.

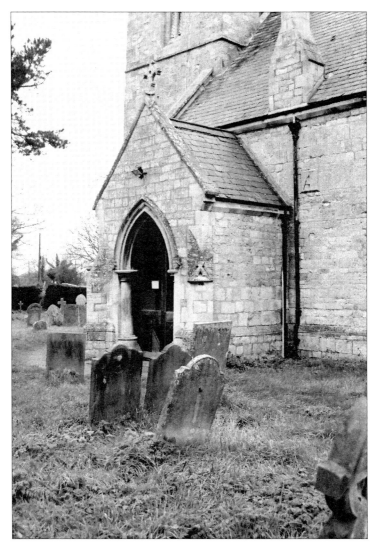

*The doorway of South Hykeham church
through which the wedding party would pass.*

17

in the Post Chaise. The woman was clearly not happy at the situation either – neither of them were. Brown hesitated no longer and ran through the ceremony, "Do you Thomas take Mary…", "Do you Mary take Thomas…" No happiness, no joy here, only people resigned to getting a job over and done with.

The ceremony over, they made their way to sign the register. Brown and the constables looked on as the newly-weds made their marks, each of them making a cross in the space where they were supposed to put their names. You can imagine what Brown was thinking as he watched them, "More illiterates, when will they ever learn to control themselves? Why couldn't they do things as they should? Save their selves, go through the joy of having the Banns read, a beautiful wedding for all to enjoy, and then the wonder of each other. No it always ends this way." Brown entered their names at the side of their marks. At the side of Thomas's cross he wrote – Thomas Temple, his mark – and at the side of the cross that Mary entered – Mary Kirkham, her mark –

no need to put anything else his job was done. Their duty complete, the constables left, there was no need to stay longer. Now they were married the parish had no need to worry about looking after an unmarried mother and her illegitimate child.

The newly-married couple left the church and started on the long walk to Lincoln some miles distant. Thomas was a man with the reputation of being malicious and revengeful, with an especially cruel streak towards animals. One particularly nasty story recalled about him was that he cut the eyes out of an ass, and with the same knife made incisions each side of its tail – he then placed the eyes into the cuts he had made. All this while the poor creature was still alive.

Maybe his childhood had been a defining factor in his behaviour, maybe not, but one thing for sure, his early years had not been easy. His father had died when he was young and he had been brought up by his uncle. But with his approaching adulthood his need for continued employment was of great importance and although he had had several jobs, he never managed to stay long in any employment. By the time he was twenty-three years-old he had found himself working as a labouring banker (or navvie), in Lincoln. It was while engaged in this work that he first met Mary Kirkham, a twenty-four year-old young woman from North Hykeham. Soon the romance blossomed and Mary became pregnant with Thomas's child. However it was apparent that this was not to be a happy occasion as Thomas clearly had no intention of marrying Mary. But for the intervention of the Magistrates the Parish, would have had to dip into their

South Hykeham as it appears today.

North Hykeham church. At the time of the marriage between Mary and Thomas, North Hykeham did not have its own church. hence the necessity to hold the ceremony at South Hykeham.

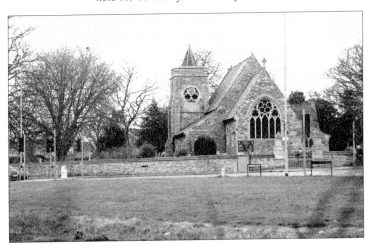

coffers to look after Mary and her child.

With the ceremony complete the rest of the day passed without incident and in the afternoon they made their way towards Saxilby, passing through the turnpike and over Saxilby drawbridge heading towards Doddington at just before six o'clock. Little did poor Mary Kirkham know that in little over an hour she would be dead. Thomas and his new bride made their way along the high road eventually turning onto the lane that runs from Drinsey Nook to Doddington. The sun had long since set and it was fortunate that the moon was out to light their way in this dark and lonely part of the countryside. It was along this lane that Thomas turned to Mary and bid her to sit down and rest. As she sat there with her head hanging down, Thomas quietly reached into the hedge behind. Using his great strength, he tore out a stake, and with both hands he brought it down with a mighty crash onto the back of Mary's head. She lurched forward letting out a cry and fell to the floor. As she lay there horribly injured and quivering, Thomas used the murderous weapon once more, this time cracking her skull to pieces. In a matter of moments, Mary was still. No more movement. Both Mary and her unborn child were dead.

The unfortunate brides' body lay in the cold all night and it wasn't until the following morning that Thomas Bowker and Daniel Fletcher discovered her body lying in the dyke on the Lincolnshire side of the lane. Soon the alarm had been raised and the locals rushed to the scene. An old cart was found and sent on its way to pick up the body. The blood-soaked murder weapon, along with one of the victim's shoes, being found nearby in the stubble close by Mary Wilson. In

Part of the Swanpool today.
It was here that Thomas Otter worked as a navvie.

Doddington village as it is today.

their hurry though, the villagers attending the gruesome scene, forgot to cover the bottom of the cart with either straw or sacking with the result that blood and gore were said to be spattered all along the Fossdyke and over Saxilby draw-bridge, as Mary's shattered body was taken back to Saxilby. It was even said that as the body passed over the bridge the Fossdyke underneath ran red. The cart pulled up outside The Sun Inn in Saxilby and her body was carried inside, with more of Mary's blood spilling onto the mounting steps and doorstep of the inn. For years afterwards the servants of John Rowe the landlord claimed that no matter what they did or tried, whether it be scrubbing or scouring the steps, the staining would soon return. Many a servant is said to have handed in their notice rather face the task again.

The following day the inquest into Mary Kirkham's death

The Sun Hotel about 1910. Viewed from the bridge, it gives the impression of what could be seen on the approach to Saxilby on the road from Doddington. Imagine the scene of 1805 as the body of Mary Kirkham was brought back to The Sun and the gathering crowds to witness the spectacle.

Another view of The Sun taken in 1904. Note the mounting steps to the left of the group outside.

The Sun Inn at Saxilby, although remodelled during the 19th century, it still retains some of its original features, including the infamous mounting steps.

The mounting steps on which the blood of Mary Kirkham spilt. For many years afterwards, the bloodstains refused to be cleaned away, and many employees left, rather than face the ordeal again.

took place in the same room within The Sun Inn, where her body had remained all the previous night. It is at this point that legend gives two possible versions of the arrest of Thomas. One story relates to how the murderer was brought to face his possible accusers by the Lincoln constables. The constables had brought Thomas under close guard in a Post Chaise to be present at the inquest of his wife, after being recognised while in Lincoln. Throughout the procedure Thomas denied all knowledge of the killing, and even when the murder weapon was placed in his hands, as the body of Mary lay on the table in front of him, he denied ever seeing it before. Unfortunately for him though, Samuel Tukes, one of the constables, who was also a butcher, was an observant man with a keen eye. As the sun shone through the window he saw the tell-tale signs of a patch of blood on the sleeve of the killer, thus sealing his fate.

Another version tells how poor Mary's body lay there at the inn as the damning evidence was heard, witnesses coming forward to give the little evidence that they knew, and even though no-one had seen the murder, the assembled jury returned a verdict of "Wilful murder against her husband Thomas Temporal." It was the following day, the sixth day of November, that Thomas was recognised and arrested in Lincoln. No matter what he said to deny his involvement, he could not escape. His accusers arrested him and took him to the castle to await trial, and if found guilty, to face his just and lawful punishment.

After the grisly but necessary inquest had done its duty, the lifeless body of Mary and her unborn were taken to St. Botolph's, Saxilby's village church, and there in the north

The interior of Saxilby church.

The north-east corner of Saxilby churchyard where Mary Kirkham and her unborn child were laid to rest on that cold November day.
The exact location of her grave has been forgotten.

*St Botolph's, Saxilby, the church where Rev Thomas Rees
led the burial service for Mary Kirkham.*

Saxilby village today.

east comer of the churchyard on that cold and solemn autumn day, they were both laid to rest, together for eternity, Thomas Rees the vicar saying a few words as the cold earth covered their mortal remains for evermore.

For weeks and months, Thomas was kept incarcerated in the gaol that lay within the castle grounds, until finally the day of his judgement loomed large. On the twelfth day of March 1806 the crowds gathered as the Lent Assizes were convened. Eager anticipation spread throughout the on-lookers as the appointed hour for its beginning drew near. A variety of cases were to be heard that day, Richard Ramsden for stealing some hams and David Dickinson for stealing sheep, were but two of them, yet the trial the crowd clamoured to hear was that of Thomas Temple. A murder trial was a sought after public event, but such a brutal

The gateway of Lincoln Castle, seen from inside the fortress.
Thomas would have passed this way to his execution.

The exterior of the castle gate.

killing brought all and sundry to hear the gruesome details. This was indeed an entertainment that couldn't be missed.

Within the full courtroom, the commanding Baron Sir Robert Graham presided over the proceedings, his dominating presence giving a powerful air throughout the room. A man of high reputation and standing, in six years time he was to reach one of the high points of his distinguished career, when he was chosen to be one of the three judges chosen to preside over the trial of John Bellingham, the assassin of Spencer Percival the British Prime Minister. The jury of twelve men good and true waited as Thomas was led before them. Without delay the trial began. For five long hours the proceedings went on. Twenty witnesses came forward to give evidence, not one of them gave evidence on behalf of the defendant. All who spoke, came to condemn the accused. Who had witnessed the murder? No-one. Who had heard the murder taking place? No-one. All the evidence given was circumstantial, but as each of the witnesses added their own testimony, the jury became more and more convinced as to guilt of the defendant. But would it be enough to convict the unrepentant Thomas? The only chance of escape for Thomas would be to have the trial dismissed on a technicality. It was claimed that the court had no jurisdiction because the body of Mary Kirkham had been found in the boundary dyke between Lincolnshire and Nottinghamshire, and so the court had no right to try him. Judge Graham shrewdly judged that the court did have the right to perform the trial. Presumably he judged rather than a boundary dyke being in neither county, it was actually in both. The jury were ordered to consider their verdict. Such was the weight of the argument presented by the prosecution, it took them but a few minutes to reach their inevitable conclusion. Sir Robert Heron the foreman pronounced the expected and inevitable verdict... "Guilty!"

Baron Graham turned towards Thomas – it was clear to all those assembled in the courtroom the sentence that would be imposed... the only sentence that could be imposed... Death! Indeed it was – the judge ordered that the sentence be death, and that afterwards his body be dissected. Everyone knew that dissection could not be part of the sentence, but after execution a body was forfeit to the state so they could in effect do as they wished. Who cared anyway? All his rights had gone the moment he had done his terrible deed, and if anything, the sentence didn't express the horror of the things he had done. Thomas was led away as composed as ever.

As the day wore on, word spread quickly, there was going to be an execution – a true spectacle that was too good to be missed. Again word spread, not one but two executions. David Dickinson had also been given the ultimate in punishments for his theft of the sheep. The expectations of the locals were already rising – a good hanging would bring in the crowds, and as well as entertainment, the hangings would bring invaluable income and trade.

Preparations were set in motion, the gallows were raised, and the tradesmen prepared their wares. Inside the gaol Thomas waited. If he could hear the hustle and bustle outside its forbidding walls, we shall never know. Perhaps now the fear was beginning to set in, perhaps only now did it dawn

The view from Lincoln Castle of the site of the gallows.

The Georgian frontage of the gaol within the castle grounds, where Thomas Otter was kept during his trial, and afterwards, awaiting execution.

on him the consequences he was about to reap for the terrible deed he had done. While Thomas sat in his cell considering his fearful future, Baron Graham, preparing himself for the journey to Nottingham to preside over the assizes there, had reconsidered his judgement. After the hanging, instead of dissection, he ordered that Thomas be gibbeted close to the scene of his terrible act. Let this punishment be a warning to others, for gibbeting was regarded by many to be the ultimate in humiliation for the body of the executed. Their remains would be secured in a framework of iron and suspended from gallows near to the scene of their crime, yet more to the point they would never rest on hallowed ground and would never find peace. Little did anyone know that Thomas would be the last person to be gibbeted in Lincolnshire. With this change in proceedings the blacksmith Gazzard was ordered to make up the gibbeting irons to fit Thomas. But such was Thomas's anger

that when Gazzard approached him to get the measurements, he was threatened with such violence that he decided it was safer to leave things be and make the irons with a mixture of experience and guesswork. The long hours passed and perhaps during this time, Thomas finally came to regret his deeds, for before he left the gaol for the last time, he confessed to the attending clergyman and the keeper of the castle his guilt.

On the fourteenth day of March, Thomas was taken from his cell within the gaol and out of the castle gate to meet his doom. For many hours the crowds had been gathering, jostling each other for the best view, trying to get the best vantage point. Thousands had turned out to see the last moments of such a sadistic killer. The noise and clamour from the assembled gathering must have been intimidating and frightening even for such a hardened character. For the first time his resolution and fortitude seemed to leave him and he made his way to the gallows with his head bowed. Alone, he made the seemingly long and endless journey to his death. Alone because David Dickinson's sentence had been commuted to transportation for life, to some, a sentence worse than death, to others a chance of living. It had become accepted that anyone who had committed a felony such as sheep-stealing for the first time would have the death sentence commuted to transportation. But now all eyes were on Thomas, and Thomas alone. The thousands in the gathered crowd watched as he finally reached the gallows. From every vantage point the baying crowd craned to see the grisly events unfold. Enterprising home owners would even rent out rooms for those with money to spare, so they could

*Lincoln Cathedral would be one of the last things
that the condemned prisoner would see as he left the castle
to make his way to the place of execution.*

Lincoln, as seen from near the Swanpool.

get a better view. Finally with the noise of the assembled tumult reaching fever pitch, the hangman's rope was placed around his neck and slowly he died the death of a murderer.

After all due ceremony had taken place, the body was taken back into the castle and there it lay until the gibbeting irons were complete. Just before ten in the morning of the twentieth day of March, after the body of Thomas had been sewn into a canvas cover, clad in pitch and then enclosed within the irons, the body was taken from the castle on a cart that made its way towards Drinsey Nook and the place of gibbeting. Many strange things were to occur that wild and windy day – some say it was the wind that was the cause of it, some say it was Thomas himself that was getting his last revenge on those that had come to gloat. Whatever the reason, it remains a fact that as the cart passed over Saxilby drawbridge, the bridge broke injuring several people. More than likely the weight of the body covered in the pitch, and irons and the huge crowd that followed, was too much of a strain for the bridge to take. Even as the cart made its way to its final destination, several people were seen to faint in the crush as they craned to get a glimpse of the body while it lay in the back of the cart. With the onlookers following, the cart finally reached the spot where the gibbet was to be erected, close to the scene of the murder. Willing hands helped to lift the body out and attach it to the thirty foot high gibbeting post which was being made ready for raising into its final position. Maybe it was the wind that made it so difficult to raise the post into its final position or maybe it was the weight of the body, but as the post was being raised up the body of Thomas fell to the ground. Once again the helpers attached the body to the gibbet and began to raise the post and once again the body fell, this time onto a poor man below. The badly injured man was taken to Drinsey Nook

House close by. So severe were his injuries, he died the following day. Even after death, Thomas was taking the life of another. Two innocent people dead because of one evil man.

Such was the interest provoked by the grisly proceedings, that booths and stalls were set up, not just for the day but for weeks afterwards, so that the area took on the appearance of a fair. Time passed slowly and Thomas' body began to decay so that before a year had gone by, a willow biter (or blue tit) had made its nest in the now gaping mouth. Soon the young could be heard inside this macabre home giving rise to two poems that arose to commemorate this strange event.

> 'The living dwell within the dead,
> The old go out to fetch the bread,
> To feed the young within the head.'

And

> 'There were nine tongues within one head,
> The tenth went out to seek for bread,
> To feed the living within the dead.'

Even as the years rolled past, the fascination with this grizzly spectacle refused to diminish. Locals would take their food with them to sit and have a picnic within sight of the slowly swinging chains. Pipe-smokers would cut off small slithers of wood from the gibbet itself to use on their pipes, while others would take a piece purely as a souvenir. Over time so much of the structure was taken that it became weakened and had to be strengthened with stays. For forty-four years the gibbet stood there giving its stark warning to all that this was the fate that awaited all those who committed the worst of crimes. For forty-four years it withstood the elements until the great storm of 1850, when it finally succumbed and came crashing to the ground. All over the area great destruction had ravaged, but it was the fallen gibbet that was still causing a stir. Locals from all around the vicinity came to take souvenirs. It is said that the constable of Saxilby took some of the gibbeting irons. Some say it was gypsies that took some, but whoever it was, soon all trace of this method of punishment was completely erased forever. One piece of the irons was rescued by the owner of Doddington Hall, Edwin Jarvis, who managed to keep it for posterity, and to this day it is on display in the Hall as a vivid reminder of a terrible event.

As the body of Thomas hung there in its chains the legend of Tom Otter began to grow, even after death his presence was ruling the lives of those around him. The first anniversary of Mary Kirkham's murder had begun to approach and memories were stirred once again, and drawn back to the events of the previous year. The murder weapon itself, far from being an object of repulsion and horror had retained a morbid fascination, and had been kept as a memento to admire and wonder at. For nearly a year it had been kept safe and was on display in the Sun Inn for all to see. The third day of November 1806 passed much the same as every other day, except for the increased buzz of conversation about the tragedy of the previous year, as many remembered the anniversary. It was the following morning

Doddington Hall, where during the 19th century, Edwin Jarvis lived. It was he who retrieved some of the gibbeting irons that had held the body of Thomas Otter for 44 years, before the gibbet was blown down in a storm. The irons are now on display in the Hall.

Doddington Church which stands close to the Hall.

41

that consternation gripped the area – the murder weapon had gone. A search of the vicinity soon found it in the same place that it had been one whole year ago to the day – in the stubble close beside the dyke on the lane to Doddington. Questions abounded – who had done it? Was it the Devil or was it Thomas come back to wreak vengeance? Year after year on the anniversary of the killing the stake would be taken from its place of keeping, and the next morning be found in the same place as it was on that first fateful day. On at least two occasions it had been secured to the wall of the inn in which it was kept, and on both occasions the iron hoops keeping it to the wall had been ripped out and the stake taken away. Whether it was kept in Saxilby or at Torksey Lock, or any other place, the result was always the same. On the anniversary of the murder, the weapon would be taken from its place of keeping. On one occasion, the securing hoops had been thrown through the window of Dick Naylor, the blacksmith, who had made them. Maybe it really was Thomas come back after all, because Dick Naylor had helped Gazzard make the gibbeting irons for the doomed Thomas.

Rumours and superstitions abounded as these unearthly proceedings continued and began to undermine the authority of the establishment, making it clear that action had to be taken to stop things getting out of hand. The Bishop of Lincoln decided that enough was enough and ordered that the hedge stake be taken to the Cathedral and burnt, even so this was done at night time, probably to avoid a conflict between believers and non-believers. Regardless of the reasoning behind this action, the desired effect was

Torksey Lock. It was at an inn, not far from here,
that the murder weapon was kept for a time, and mysteriously
disappeared on the anniversary of the murder.

The Bishop of Lincoln decided that enough was enough, and ordered that
the hedge stake be taken to the Cathedral and burnt –
even so this was done at night time,

achieved and so at last calm returned to the area.

Years passed, memories faded, and life carried on much the same as before, until one day when word began to spread... "Dunberly. John Dunberly was there. He saw it. He saw it all." For years, John Dunberly (sometimes called Dunkerly), had kept a secret to himself, unable to tell anyone out of fear for his life. But now on his deathbed the time had come to clear his conscience, so that he could meet his maker in peace. Calling for a clergyman, he gave his confession, telling everything that he had seen and heard on the night of the murder. There had been a witness to the murder, just one witness, who was so close to the killer and victim on that night that the witness could almost touch them as they rested in the lane near Drinsy Nook.

As the man of God carefully wrote down all he was told, Dunberly recalled how he had been drinking in the Sun Inn in Saxilby, deciding to make his way home to Doddington at just after six o'clock, his only companion being the moon-light as it guided his way. Making his way out of the village he met several men, who told him that they had seen Thomas and his new bride, just a few minutes earlier, making their way along that very same road. After walking for some while he had turned onto the lane that led to Doddington, but before long he pulled up, after hearing Thomas bidding Mary to sit and rest. For reasons only known to Dunberly, he decided not to pass them directly but decided to climb through the hedge into the stubble close, avoiding detection. He was so close to Thomas at one point that he could have put his arm through the hedge and touched him. In horror he watched as Thomas, using his great strength,

The interior of the Sun Inn, Saxilby.

pulled out the hedge stake, which was said to be set two feet into the ground, and callously and mercilessly beat Mary to death, giving her no chance to defend herself. Such was the sight that met his eyes, he fainted only coming round later after Thomas had left the scene. When he looked around he saw the murder weapon lying close by him in the field, and obviously, without thinking he picked it up. The stake was so covered with blood and gore that it covered his hands and got onto the sleeve of his smock. Fearful that he would be accused of the murder because it was he that had the blood on his clothes and hands, he cast the weapon aside and decided to leave the area straight away, not daring to return even to the village that he called home. For months he made his way by getting whatever work he could, wherever he could, for however long he could, eventually making his way home on the twentieth day of March – the same day as the gibbeting of Thomas. When he found out that Thomas had been tried, convicted and executed for Mary Kirkham's murder he regained some of his old confidence and joined in with securing the body of Thomas onto the gibbet post and raising it into its final position. Unfortunately for Dunberly, the securing chains on the gibbet were not as sturdy as they should have been, and when the body fell after the fixings broke, he was one of the men who was standing underneath and suffered painful injuries. As he was helped to his feet he swore that the hand of Thomas had took hold of his own and gripped it so tightly it caused marks that took many a day to disappear. Painful as his injuries were, he made light of them, even when asked what had caused them, keeping the real reason to himself.

With the gibbet and Thomas set in their final resting place, life seemed to return to normal for Dunberly. He even had the courage to walk past the swinging corpse without too much apprehension, only really fearing to go near the spot where the murder had taken place. Life carried on like this until the anniversary of the murder approached. During the day he found he had difficulty in keeping awake, and try as he might, sleep began to creep up on him, so much so that just after dusk he found he could not keep awake any longer and so went to bed. Whether it was a dream, or whether he had a vision is unclear, but he swore that before him stood Thomas who ordered him to go to the Sun Inn and retrieve the murder weapon. Full of fear and trepidation, Dunberly did as he was told, pulling the stake away from its fixings on the wall, and then making his way along the lane in a kind of twilight, back to the same spot where the killing had taken place twelve months earlier. As he travelled along, Dunberly knew he was not alone, in front of him was Thomas and behind him was Mary, both of them dressed in the same clothes as they were on that fateful night a year ago. When they approached the murder spot, events repeated themselves in the same manner that they had done that tragic first time around. Thomas bid Mary to sit and rest; she rested with her head down. But this time Thomas never lifted a finger to harm her directly. With hate in his eyes he ordered Dunberly to carry out the terrible deed, afterwards telling him to cast the hedge stake into the stubble close, mirroring the events of the previous year.

This was not the end of the matter for Dunberly – each year the same events were re-enacted, no matter where he was, he became overcome by the same feelings and no matter where the hedge stake was kept, and no matter how it was secured, he still took it and re-enacted events the same as he did every year. Only when the Bishop of Lincoln ordered the stake to be burnt did the nightmare come to an end for him. Only then did the vision of Thomas cease to haunt him and leave him in peace.

But why did Thomas kill the unfortunate Mary in the first place? The answer is quite simple – he was already married, and he seems to have thought the only way out of the second marriage was to take drastic action. It appears that he married his first wife quite legally under his real name of Thomas Otter, the couple even having a child as proof of their union. It was while his wife and child were living near Southwell in Nottinghamshire, that he met Mary and was forced into marriage because of her pregnancy. Although illiterate, he obviously wasn't stupid, so rather than be caught out as a bigamist and face possible punishment, he decided to go through with the charade of a second marriage by using an alias, and what better alias to use than his mother's maiden name of Temporal? The chances of anyone finding out that he was bigamously married were remote indeed, so his decision to murder Mary can only be put down to his renowned fiery, aggressive temperament, and this ultimately led to his downfall.

Today the lane near Drinsey Nook shows no sign of the terrible events that took place all those years ago. Progress has taken its toll on the once quiet country road, and today it is a busy road used by many people each day as they make their way to and from work, or as they travel to see

Southwell Minster

The Saracens Head, Southwell. By the time the travellers from the hostelry,
and the worshippers from the Minster, were making their way home that
dark evening of November, 1805, Mary Kirkham was already dead.

Tom Otters Lane. It was along this lane that Thomas Otter perpetrated his wicked deed. After his execution, it is where his body was gibbeted as a warning to others.

*This is the strongest contender for the site of the gibbet. No evidence exists
as to its exact whereabouts, but from the various descriptions given,
this seems the most likely place.*

Doddington and its beautiful Hall in the rolling countryside. All traces of the gibbet have long since gone, although its probable site can still be seen. The scene of the murder, too, has changed out of all recognition, yet the lane itself still retains something that raises the eyebrow of many a traveller – its name. For today, it is called Tom Otters Lane. How many people that travel upon it know of the events that led to its naming? Do they know that they pass Gibbet Wood as they go about their daily trips to work?

In Saxilby the Sun Inn is still there, remodelled in the nineteenth century but still retaining some of its original features including the mounting steps that Mary Kirkhams blood spilt upon, and if you pass through the door into this old village inn, you can imagine Mary's body lying there as the inquest took place around her. The room full of horrified and curious villagers. Today it is full of visitors laughing and joking and enjoying themselves. It was said that for years after the killing, on each anniversary, the sound of a baby crying could be heard in the front room. Who knows? Maybe it did happen, maybe it didn't, but one thing for sure, there were two innocent victims that night, and together they both rest in the north-east corner of Saxilby churchyard – Mary Kirkham and her unborn child.

CONTEMPORARY SOURCES

The marriage of Thomas Otter and
Ann Temporal, 1775, from Treswell parish register.

The baptism of Thomas Otter on 3rd March 1782,
from the Treswell parish register.

The marriage of Thomas and Mary
in South Hykeham parish register.

Record of the burial of Mary Kirkham
in the Saxilby parish register.

No 27

Timothy Learad   of [this] Parish
and _Sarah Fish_   of [this]
Parish   were
Married in this [Church] by [Banks]
this _eleventh_ Day of _October_ — in the Year One Thousand seven Hundred
and _seventy three_ — by me _J. Flint, Official Minister_
This Marriage was { _Timothy Learad_
solemnized between Us { _Sarah Fish_ + _her Mark_
In the { _Josiah Smith_
Presence of { _John Temporall_

No 28

_1774_

George Gyles —   of [this] parish _Gentleman_
and _Dorothy Learad_   of [this]
Parish — _Spinster_   were
Married in this [Church] by [Licence] —
this _fourth_ Day of _February_ — in the Year One Thousand seven Hundred
and _Seventy four_ by me _Seth Ellis Stevenson_ [Rector]
This Marriage was { _Geo: Gyles_
solemnized between Us { _Dorothy Learad_
In the { _Richard Kitchin_
Presence of { _John Temporall_

No 29

John Sidda   of [this] Parish
and _Rebecca Rose_   of [the]
Parish of _Laneham_   were
Married in this [Church] by [Banns]
this _seventeenth_ Day of _May_ in the Year One Thousand Hundred
and _seventy four_ by me _John Holmes curate of Leverton_
This Marriage was { _John Sidda_
solemnized between Us { _Rebecca Rose's_ + _Mark_
In the { _William Sidda_
Presence of { _John Temporall_

No 30

Thomas Otter   of [this] Parish a _Farmer_
and _Ann Temporal_   of [the]
parish _Spinster_   were
Married in this [Church] by [Banns] —
this _thirtieth_ Day of _July_ — in the Year One Thousand seven Hundred
and _Seventy five_ — by me _Seth Ellis Stevenson_ [Rector]
This Marriage was { _Thomas Otter_
solemnized between Us { _Ann_ + _Temporal her Mark_
In the { _Joshua Farmer_
Presence of { _Jos: Limroy_

56

Married in this [Church] by [Banns] in the Year One Thousand Hundred

this seventeenth Day of May and seventy four by me John Hobbs Curate of Treswell

This Marriage was { John Siddac /
solemnized between Us { Rebecca Bowe + Mark

In the { William Sidda
Presence of { John Temporall

No 30

of [this] Parish Farmer
and Ann Temporal — of [the] were

Thomas Otter
mark

Married in this [Church] by [Banns] in the Year One Thousand Seven Hundred
this thirtieth Day of July and seventy five by me John Ellis Newinson Rector

This Marriage was { Thomas Otter
solemnized between Us { Ann + Temporal his Mark

In the { Weston Darnell
Presence of { Job Fincher

The marriage of Thomas Otter and Ann Temporal in 1775 from the Treswell parish register.

57

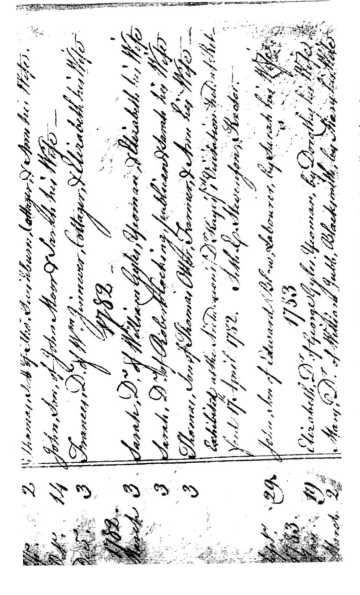

The baptism of Thomas Otter on 3rd March 1782, from the Treswell parish register.

Marriage certificate for Thomas and Mary
in the South Hykeham parish register.

* This Thomas Temple is the noted Tom Otter executed and hung in chains
for murder of Mary Kirkham.

Thomas Temple of the Parish of St Mary Wigford in the City of Lincoln and
Mary Kirkham spinster of the Parish of North Hykeham in the County of
Lincoln were married in this church by licence this third day of November
in the one thousand eight hundred and five by me
Thomas Brown Curate,

This marriage was solemnised between us:
Thomas Temple X his mark
Mary Kirkham X her mark
In the presence of Wm Shuttleworth and John Shttleworth

* The note about Thomas Otter was added at a later date.

Reproduced by kind permission of Lincolnshire Archives.

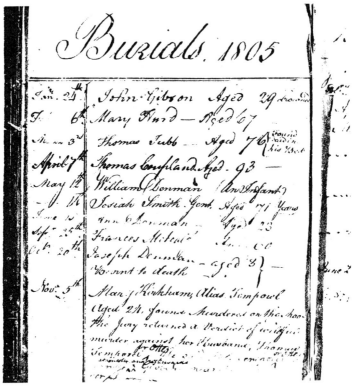

Record of the burial of Mary Kirkham in the Saxilby parish register.

Nov. 5th
Mary Kirkham alias Temporel aged 24 found murdered on the moor.
The jury returned a verdict of willful murder against her husband
Thomas Temporel (or Otter).
The said Thomas Temporel (or Otter) was hanged (at Lincoln and
afterwards) gibbeted near the place he killed her.
Burial attested by Thomas Rees Vicar
(Some of the writing was added at a later date
when the truth behind the events began to emerge)
Reproduced by kind permission of Lincolnshire Archives.